Protopresby

For parents
who DON'T know everything!

Q&A: In the light of Orthodox Christian Teaching

Baltimore 2025

Protopresbyter Georgios Oikonomou, PhD

"For parents who DON'T know everything"
Q&A: In the light of Orthodox Christian Teaching
1st ENGLISH EDITION (ADAPTED FROM THE GREEK 3rd EDITION)

Book Design & Layout: Andreas Leoudis

For central distribution in USA, Canada and Greece contact:
parentsdontknoweverything@gmail.com

Publication Date: 1/1/2025
ISBN: 979-8-9921501-0-0

Baltimore, MD, USA

Prologue

How many times has every parent found themselves in an uncomfortable position when hearing their children's questions that are too "special", "difficult", or "advanced"? This is, firstly, an attempt to codify some of these questions and, secondly, an effort to grapple with these questions in a simple, spontaneous, and heartfelt manner, as a parent would. Each child has their own unique conditions of receptivity and understanding, and these answers do not claim to offer easy or universal acceptance. More profoundly, they are directed at us as parents, so that once we have understood certain things, we can then have a dialogue with our children.

In this dialogue, it is of utmost importance to first listen with immense attention and respect to what the child is concerned about. We should also try to remain unperturbed, however difficult the question may be, in order not to "lock" the child's willingness to communicate. Additionally, it is not terrible if we are not ready to answer immediately; we can postpone the answer until another time, after preparing ourselves by studying, praying, or even seeking the advice of an expert.

This is an opportunity to thank my beloved brother in Christ, Athanasios Kanakis, who as an excellent Psychologist was kind enough to study the answers that follow and offer valuable insights. I must also thank Stelios Resvanidis for his encouragement, and personal interest in completing this effort. Finally, I thank the excellent Graphic Designer Andreas Leoudis, who meticulously approached the illustration and the entire publication of this book with perfect aesthetic sensitivity.

Fr. Georgios Oikonomou

Contents

1 Dad, can I talk to God?

Of course, my child! God is our Father. Just as I am your father, all men have God as their Father. That is why we say in our prayer, *"Our Father who art in Heaven".* As you speak with me, you can also speak with God the Father in the words of prayer. God hears our prayers with love and joy and gives us many blessings. As Christ Himself said to His Disciples, *"Ask and it will be given to you; knock and the door will be opened to you".* Thus, my child, you can talk to God!

Mom, where does someone go when they die?

When God created Adam and Eve, my child, those first humans were immortal! But they made a big mistake; they did not follow God's commandment, which was not to eat from the fruit of a tree in the center of Paradise. From that moment on, they and all of us, their descendants, lost immortality. We, as Christians, believe that when a person dies, their soul goes to Christ, to the arms of God, to Paradise. From there, from "Heaven", they see us, love us, and rejoice with us! This faith, founded on the Resurrection of Christ, by which He conquered death, gives us hope, strength, and consolation to face the loss of our loved ones who have "left" us.

3 Dad, why are we lighting a candle in church?

When the bell rings for us to go to church, God invites us to come to His house! By accepting this invitation and entering the church, we do not go "empty-handed" but offer God a small gift. In return, God offers us a Holy Gift, Holy Communion. One small gift we can offer is a candle. We light a pure and clean candle, praying to God and asking Him, if we wish, for any matter, such as giving light, health, and blessing to our family and the entire world!

4 Mom, can I see God?

Christ once said to His Disciples, *"Happy are the pure in heart, for they shall see God!"* Since all of Christ's words are true, we believe that yes, we can see God. But to see Him, we need to be able to see not only with the eyes of the body but also with the eyes of the heart. When our heart is pure, free from wickedness and sin, God Himself is revealed to us. Besides, when we worship an image of Christ, we see God. God, too, can be revealed in many ways in our lives, so we must be careful to keep our hearts pure.

5 Dad, what is the Second Coming?

The First Coming was when God became man, and Christ was born in Bethlehem. The First Coming was completed when Christ ascended into Heaven, forty days after His Holy Resurrection. Christ Himself said that He would come again, and that would be the Second Coming. He will come with glory and honor. All men who were ever born and lived in this world will stand before Him, and God will judge them. Those people who had love in their hearts and helped their fellow man will go to Heaven, while the selfish, who never helped anyone, will stay away from God in hell.

6 | Mom, can I be a saint?

One commandment that God gave to people in the Bible is to become holy. Holy is God, but He invites all people, like you, to be holy too! If you want to become a saint, you must strive to live your life according to God's will by following the path revealed by God Himself. This path is shown to us in the holy words of the Bible. All the Saints of the Church were once children like you! And they remained "children" throughout their lives, making sure their hearts were filled with love and remained pure from evil.

7 Dad, why are we kissing the priest's hand?

Priests are people to whom the Holy Church has entrusted the sacrament of the priesthood. When a baby is born and 40 days after, the priest will welcome him or her by reading the 40-day blessings. Later, he will baptize and anoint the baby, give it Holy Communion, and when the child grows up, he will marry them. In general, the priest is always close to every person, in joys and sorrows, with an abundance of love. Therefore, we express our respect, love, and gratitude to him, ask for his blessing, and kiss his hand. With these hands, the priest holds *"the Holy Gifts for the Holy People of God"*, the Holy Cup, and the Holy Chalice. By kissing his hand, we ask, and we receive his blessing.

8 Mum, does God send the rain?

In a Prophets David Psalm, we read that God created everything in wisdom. In the same Psalm (103), we learn that God sends rain as a blessing: *"From your home above you send rain on the hills and water the earth. You let the earth produce grass for cattle, plants for our food"*. Without rain, there would be no life! There would be no water to drink, neither for us humans, nor for the little animals, nor for the plants, flowers, and trees. Rain is truly a gift from God, and every time it rains, we should thank Him with gratitude.

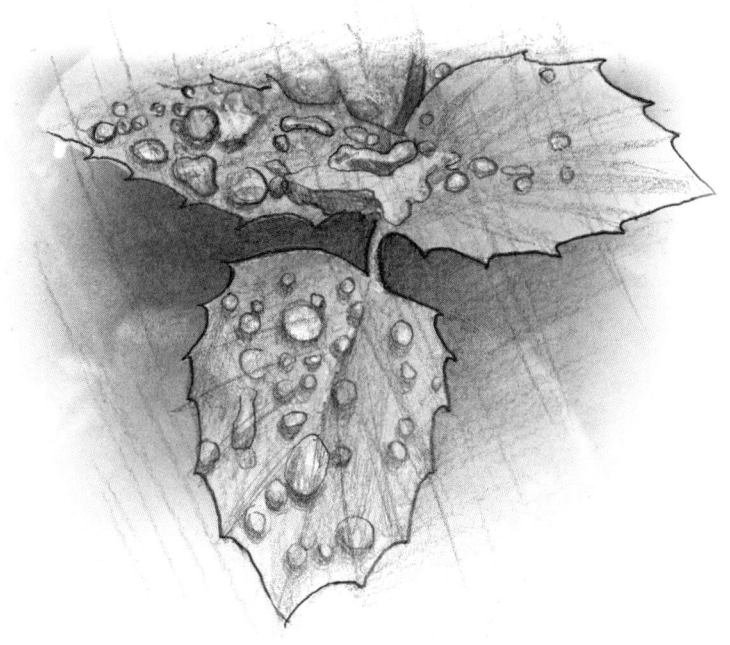

Dad, why did God take (a loved one) to Him?

The merciful God, my child, created man to live forever with Him in Paradise, to be immortal. Death exists because humans chose it, disobeying God's command not to eat the forbidden fruit. Paradise is our true homeland. We were banished because of our sin. But God, who loves us so much, sent His Son to become human, conquer death, and restore eternal life to us. When (the loved one) left us, they went to be with God in the joy of Paradise. One day, we will join them there and be together again, joyful in God's embrace. We feel sadness now, which is natural because we loved them deeply. Yet we also find strength, hope, and comfort knowing they are happy near God, returned to Paradise.

10 Mom, is God wrong?

God can do no wrong, my child, absolutely none. All His actions are an expression of His love, wisdom, and justice. He is perfect and infallible. That is why we trust in His love, and everything He allows to happen, we accept it with thanksgiving and praise.

 # Daddy, why did Jesus, if He was so strong, get crucified?

You're right, son, to ask such a question. Many people at that time were puzzled by this too, even those who were crucifying Christ said, *"If he is God, let him come down from the Cross, and then we will believe in him".* Indeed, Christ had the strength to come down from the Cross if he chose to. However, he willingly sacrificed his life out of infinite love for humanity. He died so that through His Resurrection, he could conquer death and restore eternal life to people. His power was not merely human but divine as well. He demonstrated this by rising from the grave and defeating death - a feat no mere mortal could accomplish, no matter how strong...

12 Mama, why do you keep saying "Glory to God for all things"?

When we pray to God, my child, there are three ways. One is when we ask Him about a matter. The second is when we thank Him. And the third is praise, when we say, "Glory to God". Abbot Tychon, a sanctified ascetic on Mount Athos, used to emphasize the importance of praising God by saying, *"Saying once glory to God equals a thousand Lord have mercies"*. In joy and sorrow, in blessing and in temptation, we constantly say "Glory to God", expressing our faith in Him, our trust, and our love. He is our Creator and our Father and saying "Glory to God for everything" is a way in which we honor Him.

13 Dad, does God know what we're thinking?

God, my child, is omniscient. That means He knows everything, even our most secret thoughts. Many times, Christ has revealed to people their thoughts before they could express them. Of course, this does not mean that God somehow "spies" on people's thoughts, but by knowing them, He can help us. This is why Jesus said, *"Your Father knows what you need before you ask Him for help"*, and this is why we do not need to chatter in our prayers, but only to pray from our hearts.

14 Mom, what is sin?

Sin, my child, is humanity's failure to uphold God's law and commandments. According to Christ, the most significant commandments are to love God and to love our neighbor. Therefore, the greatest sins occur when we neglect to love God and our fellow human beings. Other sins include lying, stealing, disrespecting our parents, committing murder, and feeling jealous. However, even when we sin, God continues to love us and offers forgiveness when we sincerely repent. We can seek this forgiveness through the Holy Sacrament of Confession in the church, where God absolves us of all our sins!

15 Dad, do I have a guardian Angel?

Just before you were baptized, my child, in a church service called Catechesis, the priest read a blessing asking our God, *"Send, my God, into his/her life a bright Angel to protect him/her from all evil"*. From that moment on and for the rest of your life, you have had your guardian Angel close to you, who blesses, illuminates, and protects you. We may not see him with our physical eyes, but we can feel his blessing and pray to him. The guardian Angel protects us daily from many dangers, and we must live our lives in a way that honors his presence.

16 Mom, why does God take little children up to Heaven?

A child can die for a variety of reasons, such as an accident, a medical error, or a serious and rare disease. God gives humanity the gift of life. But when His love allows such a terrible ordeal to happen, and a little child goes to Heaven, we can be sure that the child is now in the arms of God the Father and in the arms of our Holy Mother, the Theotokos. The child is neither alone nor suffering but rejoicing in the joy of Paradise. We must pray and always remember these little children with love, thanking God for the precious gift of life.

17 Dad, why don't some people believe in God?

Every person is free to believe in God if they choose to or not to believe. People who do not believe in God may have been hurt or disappointed at some point in their lives, and they might hold God responsible for what happened to them, leading them to deny Him. They might also have been taught by their parents or teachers that God does not exist. This does not mean that these people are not good or that we should not love them. Someone who is seeking God may not believe now but might believe at another time. However, faith is especially important, and people who believe in God are truly happy and blessed.

18 Mom, how can I hear what God is saying to me?

God spoke to people in simple and enlightened words. These words are written in the Bible. When we read the Bible, we can hear God's words. God can also speak in our hearts when we feel joy, love, and blessings. He speaks to us when we do good and help others, and when we pray and feel guided in our lives.

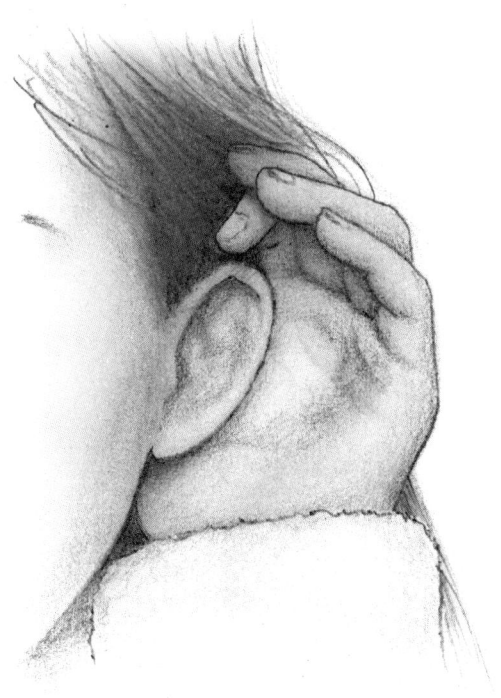

19 Dad, was Jesus a man like us?

That is right, son. He was a man like us. He was a child like you. He was born of His Blessed Mother, the Holy Theotokos, going to school, and playing with His friends. He was hungry, thirsty, ate, and did all the things we use to do. All except one: He did not sin. Because He was not only human, but He was also God. Christ existed from all eternity. He was God and He became man for our salvation. It is precisely because He became man that we feel Him so close to us, that He can understand us and help us. That is why we pray in faith to Him.

20 Mom, am I going to die?

It is true that all people will die at some point. There is no such thing as an immortal person. So, all of us will die eventually. But this is not something that should concern or frighten us too much. We have the gift of life, and this life that God has given us should be enjoyed. We should enjoy it every hour and every minute. We should live in love, joy, peace, play, and laughter. If we live our lives in this way, we will be happy, and when the time comes for us to leave this world after reaching old age, we will have lived a beautiful life. And we will continue to live, even after death, close to God in Paradise.

21   Dad, how did God make the world?

Our merciful and man-befriending God has always existed, even before the world was created. One day, His love over-flowed, and He created the world. He created it with His word: He spoke, and it was done. Thus, He made the earth and the sky, the sea and the land, the flowers and the trees, and the fish, animals, and birds that sing and give thanks to God. Everything beautiful and good, God created in His wisdom. But God's most beautiful creation was man, for He created him in His own im-age. Therefore, let us not forget to thank and praise God for His love and for all that He so beautifully created.

22 Mom, why do we make the sign of the Cross?

In Christ's lifetime, when the court sentenced a criminal to death, they would nail him to a cross and leave him there to die. It was the cruelest death. This was the harshest death that Christ, our God, was punished with. But because He went up on the Cross and sanctified it with His blood, from that time on, the Cross became a symbol of salvation. For after the Holy Cross came the Holy Resurrection. So, when we make the sign of the Cross, we honor Christ's sacrifice, we confess our faith in Him, and we receive great strength and blessing. Finally, in making the sign of the Cross with care and reverence, we remember how great Christ's love is for us, as that love went even unto death.

23 Dad, are we all children of God?

Yes, son. God is the Father of all people, and therefore all people are His children. Since we have the same Father, we are brothers and sisters to each other. Some people may be white, red, yellow, or black; some may be American, European, Asian, African, but we are all God's children. God loves and blesses all people. That is why the Bible often says that God blesses all nations. And if some nations or people have not yet believed in the true God, we always pray in love for the entire world.

24 Mom, how can God be everywhere?

In a prayer of the church, we say that God is *"present in all places and filling all things"**. This means that He is everywhere. This is because God is spirit and is not limited by the dimensions we understand, such as space and time. We can only be in one place, but God is simultaneously in Heaven and on earth, in the depths of the sea, and throughout the whole universe. Since God is everywhere, we can say that every place is holy and blessed. Wherever we find ourselves, we can pray to God, knowing that He is present and hears our prayers.

---

* *"Heavenly King, Comforter, Spirit of Truth, present in all places and filling all things, treasury of good things and giver of life: come; take Your abode in us; cleanse us of every stain, and save our souls, O Good one".*

25 Dad, where is God's house?

As we mentioned in the previous answer, God is not confined to just one place or one house; He is everywhere. However, the holy temple, the church, is especially considered to be God's house, His home. The church is a holy and sanctified place where the sacraments and the Divine Liturgy are celebrated. It is where God is definitely present, and it is indeed His house. He invites us all, opening the door of His house to welcome us and commune with Him. Therefore, whenever we go to church, we should enter with great reverence and participate in the sacraments with great care and prayer.

26 Mom, does Jesus always see what we do?

It is true that Jesus always sees what we do, as He is everywhere. The fact that He always sees our actions is a blessing and brings us joy. He watches over us out of love and often protects us. Even when we make mistakes, He sees us with sorrow but not anger. He patiently waits for us to repent and to try correcting our faults and sins. When we face difficulties, He extends His hand to lift us up. If we lose our way, He searches for us and rescues us. His constant watch over us reveals His care, His fatherly love, and His concern.

27 Dad, where is Heaven?

Heaven, my child, in the old days when God made the world, was here on earth. The entire earth was Paradise. Because Paradise means being close to God, living with Him. But now Paradise is in a place we cannot see, even with the best telescopes exploring the most distant stars and galaxies. The Church tells us that Paradise is in Heaven, meaning there is still a blessed place full of light and love, where people live eternally with God, the Holy Theotokos, the Saints, and all good people. While we don't know exactly where it is, we know it exists because Christ himself told us so in the Gospel.

28 Mom, where is the Hell?

The word "hell" (κόλαση) in Greek language means punishment. And that punishment is living away from God - away from the light, the love, the joy, the hope that He offers. Like Paradise, we do not know exactly where it is, but we are certain that it is far, far away from both Heaven and God. May all people be good, so that hell one day will be "closed" to everyone, and so that no one will ever go there again.

29 Dad, what is Heaven?

Heaven is the Kingdom of God. Here on earth, the world is governed by Presidents, senators, governors, mayors, and others. In heaven, God is the one and only Heavenly King. The "rulers" are the Archangels, Angels, Saints, Apostles, Prophets, and Martyrs. The citizens of Paradise are all righteous people who have strived in their lives to do good - to help their fellow humans, to feed the poor, to support the oppressed, to love everyone. As a reward, God grants these people eternal life close to Him in Heaven.

30 Mom, what is the Hell?

Hell is a place of suffering and despair. It's the consequence for those who have done wrong in their lives. When hungry people asked them for help, they turned them away. Others begged for a glass of water, but they refused. They never gave clothing to warm those who were cold. They treated strangers with cruelty. Despite opportunities, they neglected to care for the sick who needed help. Throughout their lives, they chose to do evil and never sought forgiveness from God.

31 Dad, why do we pray before we go to sleep?

Every night, before we go to sleep, we say good night to our parents and siblings, and then we rest. This prepares us to start a new day the next morning. When we pray before going to sleep, we talk to God, our Father who art in Heaven. We thank Him for the day that has passed, for all the blessings and joys we experienced. We also ask Him to grant us a good night's sleep without bad dreams, so that we can wake up the next day with enthusiasm and joy. Our prayers are like saying "good night" to our Father in Heaven. Through prayer, God gives us peace and serenity.

32 Mom, why do we pray before we eat?

Uncountable people, including many children around the world, unfortunately, have no food to eat and go hungry or try to ease their hunger with truly little food. We, thankfully, always have food on our table. So, we pray to thank God and ask Him to bless our meal. The time of eating is a sacred and blessed time because we are consuming the food provided to us by the love of the merciful God. That is why it is important to always say our prayers before we eat.

33 Dad, why do we pray after we eat?

As soon as we get up from the table, whether we have had breakfast, lunch, or dinner, we always say our prayers. We thank God for all the good things He has given us and for filling our table with delicious food. Just as Christ blessed the food when He ate with His Disciples, we ask Him to bless our food and multiply it. This means we pray for God's blessing so that there may be enough food for everyone in the world, especially for the poor, and so that no one goes hungry.

34 Mom, why don't we see God?

But we do see Him! We can see God every day! For example, when we look at an image of Christ, we are not just seeing a painting. When we cross ourselves and kiss the holy icon, we receive His blessing as if we were worshiping Christ Himself standing in front of us. But there is another way to see God every day! Jesus once said that we can see the face of God in the face of every fellow human being in need. When we give food to someone who is hungry, water to someone who is thirsty, clothes to someone who is cold, shelter to someone who has nowhere to stay, or visit someone who is sick or imprisoned, we are helping Christ Himself. For every person is a living image of God.

35 Dad, can Jesus help us?

Jesus once said, *"Ask and it will be given to you; seek and you will find; knock and the door will be opened to you"*. All of Christ's words are true, including the above. Certainly, Christ can help us because He is Almighty. He can assist us incomparably more than humans can, for if He desires, He can even perform miracles. The prerequisite, however, for Christ to help us is that we believe in Him and ask for His help with faith, hope, humility, and prayer. Then we can be confident that He will hear us and assist us.

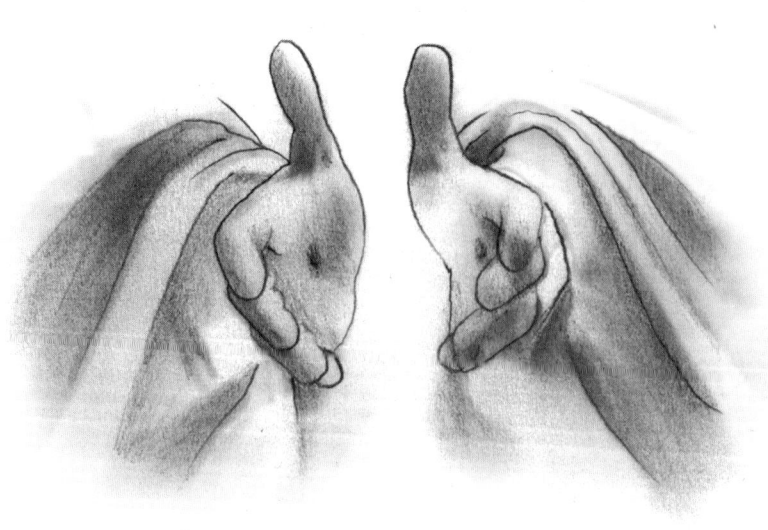

36 Mom, why do we have to go to church?

We go to church, my child, not because we "have to", but because we want to and need to. The church is God's house, where we pray, meet Him, and commune with Christ. We go there freely, responding to the "ding-dong" of the bell as an invitation. It is Christ who calls all believers to come together, to pray, and to thank Him for all the good things He blesses us with in life. Participating in the celebration, for the worship of the Church is a beautiful and glorious celebration of God, the Virgin Mary, and the Saints. When we worship, we are filled with joy and blessings.

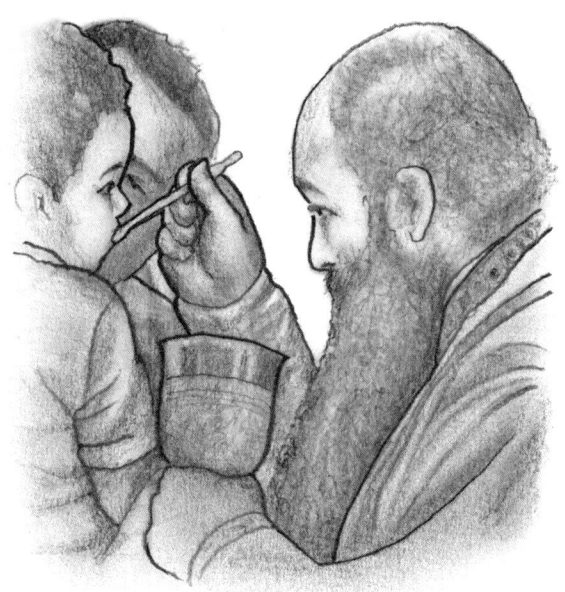

37 Dad, will God punish us if we do something wrong?

All people may do something bad at some point in our lives. However, God does not get angry or punish us because God is love. Instead, He can feel sorry for us. That is why as soon as we realize we have done something wrong, we should ask God for forgiveness at the first opportunity. In fact, the Church offers a sacrament called "Holy Confession", where we ask God for forgiveness for our mistakes, and God forgives us no matter how big our mistakes were. Therefore, we should not be afraid of being punished by God but rather try our best not to disappoint Him.

38 Mom, why do we have to turn the other cheek if someone hits us?

During the time when Christ lived, people were often cruel. When someone was hit, the common response was to seek revenge and cause even more harm. However, Christ aimed to teach people about peace, love, and forgiveness. When He said, *"If someone hits you, turn the other cheek"*, He did not mean that we should passively accept being hurt without protest. Rather, He taught us to avoid responding with anger because violence only begets more violence. Instead, we should strive to forgive those who have hurt us. Nevertheless, this does not mean we should tolerate being mistreated. It is important to assert ourselves and promptly discuss such incidents with our parents.

39 Dad, can (deceased loved one) see us from up there?

Our beloved ..., who departed from us leaving us filled with sorrow, is now close to God. They rejoice in Heaven, beholding the glory and light of God, Our Lady, the Angels, and the Saints, and are surrounded by other righteous and good people. From above, they can also see us; they are proud of us, rejoicing in our progress. In times of both wellness and adversity, they pray to God to aid us. They will always remain close to us, in our hearts, in our love, and in our prayers. We will forever cherish beautiful memories of them and carry their blessing.

40 Mom, is God angry with us?

God, my child, is not angry. We are His children, and He loves us so much that He always forgives our mistakes and sins. If God were truly angry with us, our world would not exist; it would be destroyed. Because many times we humans have made great mistakes, lived contrary to God's holy will, violated His laws and commandments, and committed great sins such as wars and injustices. Despite all these things, God is sorrowful but always gives us the opportunity to repent. We can change our lives, ask for forgiveness, and begin anew in our spiritual journey!

41 Dad, what is a miracle?

A miracle is a great blessing from God, an unexpected gift. Many miracles of God are written in the Bible, both before and after Christ came to earth. For example, one significant miracle before Christ was when the Egyptian army was pursuing the Israelites and the Red Sea was parted, allowing God's people to pass through and be saved. Even after Christ, Jesus performed many miracles. Blind people received sight, the paralyzed walked, and lepers were cleansed. But the greatest miracle of all is the resurrection of Christ! Miracles continue to happen today! When a person prays fervently to God in deep faith, asking for something, often God answers that prayer with a miracle!

42 Mom, who brings us the babies?

The first humans who lived on earth, Adam, and Eve, are our distant ancestors and were created by God Himself. God blessed them to live together in marriage and encouraged them to have many children, which they did. Since then, every baby born is seen as a blessing and gift from God to its parents and siblings, bringing them extraordinary joy. When God sees that a man and a woman have deep love and are ready to be loving parents, He blesses them with a baby!

Note: The answer to this question can vary depending on the child's personality, maturity, and how they ask the question. Approaching the topic from a biological perspective alone can sometimes be as challenging as the fanciful stories children might hear from each other. It is crucial to emphasize that God is the Creator and that a child's birth is a result of the deep love and desire of their parents to have a child. For older children who are more knowledgeable, it is important to clarify that there's nothing wrong or sinful about the marital relationship, as it is blessed by God in the sacrament of Marriage. This approach avoids the need for narratives like "babies are brought by the stork", which can lead to confusion and further questions needing clarification.

43 Dad, are God and the devil fighting?

No, son! God does not quarrel with anyone because God is love. He does not even quarrel with the devil. Instead, He teaches us through this that we should not quarrel with anyone either. God is incomparably superior to the devil; He is the Creator of Heaven and earth, the Poet of all things. The devil, on the other hand, is not a creator but a creature. Therefore, God rules the world, governs it with love, cares for it, and blesses it. The devil has no such power and authority. His only aim is to turn us away from God and to sow sinful thoughts in our minds. But we will not yield to him! We will obey only the holy will of God our Father and not the evil promptings of the devil.

44 Mom, who is the devil?

The devil was once a bright angel named Lucifer. God created him along with the other angels. However, he became proud and desired to surpass God. Therefore, God regretted his actions and allowed Lucifer to no longer be an angel but to become a devil, the Satan. He lost his position. Since then, the devil has been filled with malice and anger, attempting to lead people into sin. He tempted Adam and Eve, leading them to sin and consequently leaving Paradise. He continues to pursue the same goal. However, the devil has no power or authority before God because our God is Almighty! Therefore, we should not fear him either, because we are always protected by God's love.

45 Dad, why do some people believe in another God?

In the very first days of human history, all people believed in the same God, the true God of the Christian faith, the Creator of the entire world, the Holy Trinity. But as the years went by, some people turned away from the law and the will of the true God, living without a relationship with Him. Slowly, they made false gods, idols, or products of their imagination, and worshipped them as if they were true gods. That is how many different religions were created. Every child, when he is born, is taught by his parents to speak a language, that he belongs to a nation, and to a religion. That is why some people believe in another god. We, as Christians, must love these people, even though they belong to another religion, and be a good example so that they appreciate the importance of the Christian faith.

46 Mom, are there other gods?

No, son. God is only one. One God, the Holy Trinity. He is the one true God, the Creator of the universe. The other gods that some people believe in, such as the twelve gods of Olympus, are false, created by men in their minds. The one and only true God was revealed in human history. He became man, was born of the Virgin Mary the Holy Theotokos, taught men, was crucified, and is risen from the dead. He Himself told us that there are no other gods and that we must believe in the one God.

47 Dad, can I talk to Jesus?

The people who lived in the time of Christ, like His Disciples, were truly fortunate and blessed! They could see Christ, hear Him, and talk with Him. After Christ's Ascension to Heaven, we Christians, who are also now His disciples and students, cannot talk with Him as His contemporaries did, but we can in another way. We speak with Christ through our prayer, and Christ answers us in His Word, which are the holy words of the Bible. There are answers to all our questions there, answered by Christ Himself. Also, Christ can reveal Himself to man in many other ways, even revealing Himself, as He once appeared to Saint Paisios the Athonite when he was a child.

48 Mom, what is the Small Blessing of the Waters?

The Blessing of the Waters is one of the most beautiful sacred services. The first sanctification and Blessing of the Waters took place when Christ was baptized by John in the Jordan River, and all the waters were sanctified as Jesus Christ Himself was immersed in them. Every time a priest performs this service, we remember that first consecration and ask God, as He did then, to sanctify the water that we humbly offer to Him. Then, when the priest sprinkles us and when we drink from the holy water, we receive the blessing and are sanctified ourselves. We usually celebrate the holy water whenever we start something new, such as a new school year or a new month, to ask for God's blessing and help.

49 Dad, how should I pray?

Pray, my child, from your heart, with deep faith and filled with love for God. Pray with humility, asking for God's forgiveness for your mistakes and sins. When we pray, we do not need to say too many words, for God, as our Father, knows beforehand what we need. It is enough to say in our prayer, "Lord have mercy". Every prayer of the church has its beauty. However, the greatest prayer is the one that Christ Himself taught us. It is the perfect prayer, and we can pray it all the time with these words:

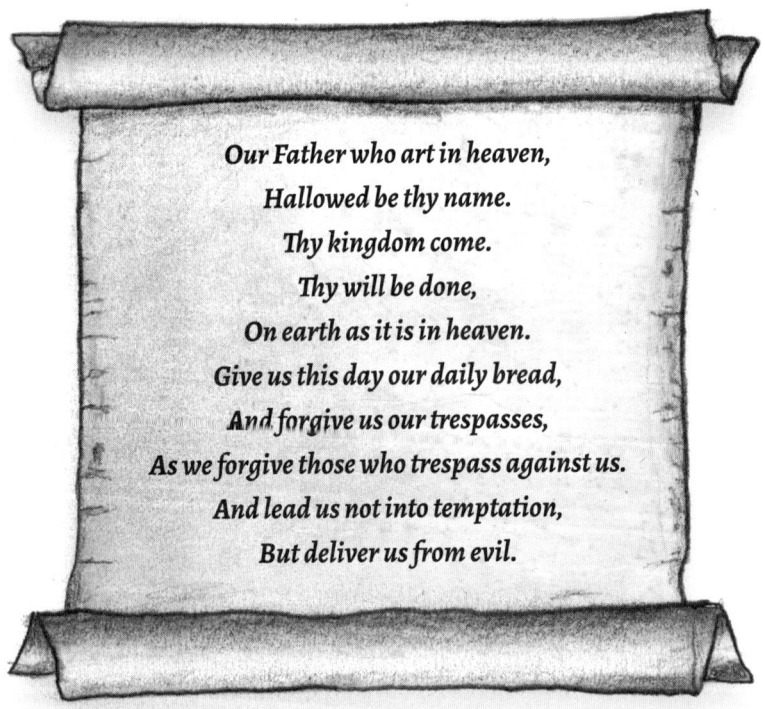

Our Father who art in heaven,
Hallowed be thy name.
Thy kingdom come.
Thy will be done,
On earth as it is in heaven.
Give us this day our daily bread,
And forgive us our trespasses,
As we forgive those who trespass against us.
And lead us not into temptation,
But deliver us from evil.

Epilogue

As parents, we often find ourselves navigating an ocean of questions - some simple, some profound, and others that challenge us to the very core of our understanding. This book is a testament to the beauty and complexity of those questions, posed by the children we hold so dear. Their inquiries reflect a genuine yearning for truth, connection, and faith.

In the light of Orthodox Christian teaching, these answers are not final declarations but invitations to dialogue, reflection, and growth. They remind us that the role of a parent is not to be infallible but to be loving, patient, and open-hearted. The journey of parenthood, much like faith, is a continuous path of learning and striving.

My prayer is that this book serves as a beacon for parents and children alike, guiding them through the moments of wonder and uncertainty, anchoring them in love and understanding. Let us never forget that in the questions of our children, we often find the answers to our own hearts.

May God bless every family with wisdom, peace, and the courage to embrace life's questions with faith and love.